MAC & CHEESE GENIUS

TIPS FROM THE CHEESE

- When possible, buy a freshly cut block of cheese from a meat counter or deli and shred it yourself so you're certain it's as fresh as possible. Not an option? Then go ahead and purchase a prepackaged block or even a preshredded bag if you must.

- Not all cheese types are created equal. Some melt smoothly *(cheddar & Gruyère, for example)*, some are stretchy and stringy when they melt (think mozzarella & provolone); and some just aren't good melters *(feta, for instance – use them anyway, but be selective in how you use them so you're not disappointed)*.

- Don't spend another day without mouth-watering mac & cheese!

Printed in the United States of America
by G&R Publishing Co.

Distributed By:

CQProducts

507 Industrial Street
Waverly, IA 50677

ISBN-13: 978-1-56383-425-1
Item #7131

Say it...
with cheese

FLAVOR. If you think that all mac & cheese is created equal, step away from the prepackaged stuff. We'll show you jacked-up flavors and serving ideas you may have only dreamed of.

VERSATILITY. Need a side dish? Go with mac & cheese. A meal idea? Mac & cheese is the answer. With these recipes, you could enjoy a different mac & cheese every day for a month. Would you want to? Um, yes!

HAPPINESS. Mac & cheese just makes people happy. Plain and simple.

YUMMINESS. Creamy and dreamy. Rich and delicious. Scoop-it-up-as-fast-as-possible heaven in a bowl.

Need more convincing? Simply turn the page.

STUFFED BELLS

- 1 lb. small frozen Italian meatballs
- 16 oz. uncooked pasta *(we used rotini)*
- 5 T. butter, divided
- ¼ C. flour
- 2¾ C. milk
- ¾ C. each shredded Gouda, Havarti & sharp cheddar cheeses
- ¼ tsp. each dry mustard & cayenne pepper
- Salt & black pepper to taste
- 1 (24 oz.) jar marinara sauce
- 10 bell peppers, any color
- ¾ C. crushed Ritz crackers
- Olive oil

Bake meatballs according to package directions. Cook pasta to al dente according to package directions; drain and rinse with cold water. Set all aside.

Preheat the oven to 400°. Melt ¼ cup butter in the empty pasta saucepan over medium heat. Whisk in the flour and cook for 1 minute, stirring constantly. Gradually whisk in milk and increase the heat to medium-high; bring to a boil, whisking frequently until slightly thickened. Remove from the heat and add all three cheeses, dry mustard, cayenne pepper, salt, and black pepper, stirring until the cheese is melted. Carefully stir in the cooked pasta and baked meatballs.

Spread the marinara sauce over the bottom of one or two greased baking pans. Cut the tops off the peppers and remove the seeds; discard the pepper tops or tuck them into the baking pans. Arrange the peppers on the marinara sauce and fill each with some of the pasta mixture.

Melt the remaining 1 tablespoon butter and stir in the cracker crumbs; sprinkle evenly over the peppers. Drizzle each with a little oil.

Cover the pan with foil and bake for 20 minutes. Remove the foil and bake 15 to 20 minutes longer or until the crumbs are toasted and the peppers have softened *(baking time may vary depending upon the size of your peppers).*

BAYSIDE MAC

½ C. butter, divided

¼ C. sliced green onions

¼ C. flour

3 C. milk

1 to 2 T. Old Bay seasoning

¼ tsp. crushed red pepper flakes

2½ C. each shredded mild & sharp cheddar cheeses

2 tsp. Dijon mustard

16 oz. uncooked pasta *(we used shells)*

1 lb. chunk-style crabmeat

¼ tsp. each garlic salt & coarse black pepper

½ C. each panko bread crumbs & coarsely crushed oyster crackers

Zest of 1 lemon

¼ C. finely chopped fresh parsley

Preheat the broiler. Grease a 3-quart baking dish; set aside.

In a big saucepan over medium heat, melt ¼ cup butter and add the green onions. Cook for 1 minute. Whisk in the flour and cook for a couple of minutes, stirring constantly. Gradually whisk in the milk, Old Bay seasoning, and pepper flakes; simmer 10 minutes, until slightly thickened, stirring often. Add both cheeses and the mustard, stirring until melted; cover.

Meanwhile, cook pasta to al dente according to package directions; drain and add to the cheese sauce. Stir in the crabmeat, garlic salt, and black pepper; transfer to the prepped baking dish.

Melt the remaining ¼ cup butter. Stir in the bread crumbs, cracker crumbs, lemon zest, and parsley; sprinkle over the pasta mixture and broil for a few minutes, until nice and brown.

SERVES 4

SPINACH & SMOKED GOUDA

Cook 8 oz. pasta *(we used rings)* until al dente according to package directions; drain. In the meantime, melt 3 T. unsalted butter in another saucepan.

Chop ½ yellow onion and add it to the butter along with ½ tsp. each coarse salt and black pepper; cook over medium-low heat for 8 minutes or until translucent. Add 2 T. flour and cook for 1 minute, whisking constantly. Slowly add 1¾ C. milk and cook about 5 minutes or until thickened, stirring occasionally. Add 8 oz. shredded smoked Gouda cheese, cover, and heat until the cheese melts, stirring often *(smoked Gouda takes a while to melt, so be patient)*. Stir in the cooked pasta and a big handful of fresh baby spinach.

MINI MAC BITES

Preheat the oven to 375°. Grease mini muffin pans.

Cook 8 oz. pasta *(we used small shells)* to al dente according to package directions; drain and return to saucepan. Stir in 4 beaten eggs, 1 C. shredded carrots, ½ C. ricotta cheese, ½ C. milk, 2 C. shredded cheddar cheese, 1 (3 oz.) pkg. bacon bits, 1½ T. dried minced onion, ½ tsp. salt, and ¼ tsp. black pepper.

Transfer the mixture to the muffin pan compartments, using ⅛ C. for each. Sprinkle with a little Parmesan cheese. Bake for 12 to 15 minutes or until the edges are brown. Let stand for a few minutes before removing from the pan.

THAI LETTUCE WRAPS

12 oz. uncooked pasta
(we used campanelle)

3 C. milk

½ C. plus 2½ T. unsalted
butter, divided

½ C. flour

2 tsp. coarse salt

1 T. minced fresh
gingerroot

2 C. shredded Havarti
cheese

2 to 3 T. Sriracha sauce,
plus more for serving

Lettuce leaves

Shredded carrots

Chopped green onions

Cook pasta according to package directions, 1 minute less than al dente. Drain and rinse with cold water. In the meantime, bring the milk to a simmer in a medium saucepan. Set everything aside.

Melt ½ cup butter in the empty pasta saucepan; add ½ cup flour and whisk for a minute or so, until it begins to brown. Slowly pour the warm milk into the flour mixture, whisking constantly over medium-high heat until silky and thickened. Stir in salt and remove from the heat.

In a small bowl, mash together the gingerroot and the remaining 2½ tablespoons butter and add it to the thickened sauce. Add the cheese, stirring until nearly melted. Stir in the Sriracha sauce and cooked pasta.

Divide the pasta mixture among lettuce leaves and top with carrots and green onions. Drizzle with more Sriracha sauce if you'd like. Fold and eat.

RAGIN' CAJUN KIELBASA

- 1 (13 oz.) pkg. kielbasa, cubed
- 2 T. olive oil
- 1 onion, chopped
- 1 green bell pepper, chopped
- ¾ tsp. salt
- ¼ tsp. black pepper
- 16 oz. uncooked pasta *(we used mostaccioli)*
- 1 tsp. minced garlic
- 1 T. flour
- 1¾ C. milk
- 4 oz. cream cheese, cubed
- 2 tsp. Cajun seasoning
- 8 oz. each shredded Gruyère & extra sharp cheddar cheeses

Preheat the oven to 425° and grease six individual ramekins.

Brown the kielbasa in 1 tablespoon oil in a big skillet over medium-low heat; use a slotted spoon to remove the kielbasa from the pan and set on paper towels to drain. Heat the remaining 1 tablespoon oil in the empty skillet and add the onion, bell pepper, salt, and black pepper; cover and cook for 8 to 10 minutes or until the vegetables are very tender, stirring occasionally. In the meantime, cook pasta to al dente according to package directions; drain.

Add the garlic to the cooked vegetables and heat for 1 minute. Sprinkle with flour and cook 1 minute longer, stirring constantly. Stir in the milk and bring to a simmer. Add the cream cheese and Cajun seasoning, stirring until nearly smooth. Stir in both cheeses and simmer until nearly melted, stirring occasionally.

Add the cheese sauce to the cooked pasta and stir in the browned kielbasa; divide among the prepped ramekins. Bake for 10 to 12 minutes or until lightly browned.

CREAMY CHICKEN & MUSHROOMS

8 oz. uncooked pasta
  (we used elbows)

2 T. vegetable oil

1 onion, chopped

1 carrot, chopped

½ red bell pepper, diced

2 chicken thighs, skinned,
  boned & cubed

1 head broccoli,
  cut into florets

8 oz. sliced mushrooms

2 cloves garlic, grated

1 (8 oz.) tub cream cheese
  spread

2 T. milk

1 T. chicken bouillon
  powder or granules

¾ C. shredded Parmesan
  cheese, divided

Preheat the oven to 400°. Cook pasta according to package directions; drain and dump into a greased 2-quart casserole dish. Set aside.

Meanwhile, heat the oil in a large skillet and add the onion, carrot, and bell pepper, cooking until onion is translucent. Add the chicken, broccoli, and mushrooms, and cook until the chicken is brown and the broccoli is crisp-tender. Stir in the garlic, cream cheese spread, milk, and bouillon powder. When the mixture begins to simmer, remove it from the heat and stir in ½ cup Parmesan cheese.

Add the mixture to the cooked pasta and stir to combine. Sprinkle the remaining ¼ cup Parmesan cheese over the top. Bake for 15 to 20 minutes, until the top has browned nicely.

TURKEY MAC TACOS

Prepare 1 (7.25 oz.) pkg. macaroni & cheese dinner mix according to package directions, stirring in 1 tsp. taco seasoning. Heat 10 corn taco shells according to package directions. Meanwhile, in a skillet, brown ½ lb. ground turkey, breaking it apart as it cooks. Stir in 1 T. plus 1 tsp. taco seasoning and 2 T. water; cook until the water evaporates.

Mix the turkey and the macaroni & cheese until well blended; divide evenly among the warm taco shells. Serve with your favorite taco toppings.

DRESSED-UP EASY MAC

Preheat the oven to 350°. Prepare 1 (5.5 oz.) pkg. macaroni & cheese dinner *(we used one with spiral pasta)* according to package directions. Meanwhile, in a small bowl, mix ¾ C. soft bread crumbs with 2 T. grated Parmesan cheese, 1 T. chopped fresh parsley, and 1 T. melted butter; set aside.

In a big bowl, stir together prepared macaroni & cheese with 1 C. cubed cooked ham, 1 C. cottage cheese, ½ C. sour cream, 1 sliced green onion, 1 (2 oz.) jar diced pimientos *(drained)*, ¼ tsp. salt, and ¼ tsp. dry mustard. Transfer to a greased 1½-quart baking dish and sprinkle with the set-aside crumbs. Bake for 25 to 30 minutes.

VEGGIE PASTA BAKE

4 medium carrots, quartered

1 head cauliflower,
  stem removed

1 C. vegetable stock

2 oz. cream cheese, cubed

1 tsp. Dijon mustard

Pinch of cayenne pepper

¾ C. shredded fontina or
  provolone cheese

½ tsp. each salt & black
  pepper

12 oz. uncooked pasta
  (we used linguini)

2 to 3 C. small broccoli
  florets

2 plum tomatoes, chopped

¼ C. grated Parmesan
  cheese

Preheat the oven to 400° and grease six individual ramekins;
set aside.

Heat a large saucepan of salted water over high heat until
boiling. Add the carrots and cauliflower head; cover and cook
for 15 to 20 minutes or until very tender. Don't drain.

In a blender, combine the stock, cream cheese, mustard,
cayenne pepper, fontina cheese, salt, and black pepper.
With a slotted spoon, transfer the cooked vegetables to the
blender *(save cooking water)*. Puree until smooth; set aside.

Add the pasta *(break in half first if you'd like)* to the cooking
water and cook according to package directions, adding the
broccoli halfway through cooking; drain and return to the
saucepan. Stir in the pureed sauce and tomatoes.

Transfer to the prepped ramekins. Top with Parmesan cheese.
Bake for 15 to 20 minutes or until heated through. Or skip the
baking and serve it immediately after you take it off the stove.

HAND PIES

- 2 (15 oz.) pkgs. refrigerated pie crust
- 8 oz. uncooked pasta *(we used rotini)*
- 2 T. butter
- ½ onion, chopped
- ½ red bell pepper, chopped
- 1 tsp. minced garlic
- 1½ T. flour
- 1½ C. milk
- 2½ C. shredded Colby Jack cheese
- 1 egg, beaten
- Black pepper & grated Parmesan cheese to taste

Preheat the oven to 425°. Line two baking sheets with parchment paper and remove the pie crusts from the refrigerator. Cook pasta according to package directions, 1 minute less than al dente; drain and return to the pan. Set all aside.

Meanwhile, in a medium skillet over medium heat, melt the butter; add the onion and bell pepper and cook for 7 minutes or until softened. Toss in the garlic and stir for 1 minute, then whisk in the flour until thick. Gradually add the milk, stirring until smooth and thickened.

Pour the thickened sauce into the cooked pasta, stirring to coat well. Add the Colby Jack cheese, a handful at a time, stirring until melted.

Cut an 8" round from one crust using a bowl or cookie cutter; reroll the scraps to make another round. Repeat with the remaining three crusts. Put a mound of the pasta mixture *(about ¾ cup)* toward one side of each round and flatten slightly; fold the crust over the filling and seal the edges with a fork. Brush with egg and sprinkle with black pepper and Parmesan cheese.

Arrange the pies on the prepped baking sheets and use a sharp knife to make a small slit in the top of each. Bake for 20 minutes or until golden brown.

SURPRISE INSIDE MEATBALLS

1½ lbs. lean ground beef

2 T. finely chopped onion

1 egg

⅓ C. panko bread crumbs

½ C. shredded cheddar
cheese

1 tsp. salt

½ tsp. black pepper

1 tsp. garlic powder

½ tsp. ground cumin

1 C. leftover chilled
macaroni & cheese
*(try one of your favorites
from this book)*

10 (½") cubes cheddar
cheese

2 T. barbecue sauce

Preheat the oven to 375°. Line a rimmed baking sheet with
parchment paper and set aside.

Stir together the ground beef, onion, egg, bread crumbs,
shredded cheese, salt, black pepper, garlic powder, and
cumin until just combined. Divide mixture into 10 even
portions and flatten each one.

Put an equal amount of macaroni & cheese in the center of
each flattened meat portion and add one cheese cube. Fold
up the sides of the meat to form a ball and pinch the edges
to seal in the filling.

Arrange the meatballs on the prepped baking sheet and
brush each with some barbecue sauce. Bake about
25 minutes or until the internal temperature reaches 160°.

CHILI MAC

1 lb. lean ground beef

½ red onion, chopped

1 tsp. minced garlic

Salt & black pepper
to taste

1 (15 oz.) can petite diced
tomatoes

1 (6 oz.) can tomato paste

1 (15 oz.) can black beans,
drained & rinsed

4 C. beef broth

1 T. chili powder

2 tsp. ground cumin

1 tsp. each paprika &
dried cilantro

½ tsp. dried oregano

2 C. uncooked pasta
(we used big elbows)

2 C. shredded sharp
cheddar cheese, plus
more for serving

Corn chips

Cook ground beef, onion, and garlic in a big saucepan over medium-high heat until beef is no longer pink, breaking it apart while it cooks; drain and return to the skillet. Season with salt and black pepper.

Add tomatoes, tomato paste, black beans, broth, chili powder, cumin, paprika, cilantro, and oregano to the saucepan. Bring the mixture to a boil and then stir in the pasta. Cook for 5 to 7 minutes or until pasta is just al dente, stirring once.

Add the cheese, stirring until melted; remove from the heat, cover, and let stand for 10 minutes.

Top with corn chips and more cheese.

SERVES 6

ONE-POT GNOCCHI

Melt 1 T. butter in a skillet. Add ½ chopped onion and cook over medium heat until soft and golden-colored. Add ½ lb. diced ham and cook until it begins to brown. Pour in ½ C. chicken broth and ¾ C. water. Increase the heat to medium-high and cook until the mixture begins to simmer.

Carefully dump in 1 (17.6 oz.) pkg. potato gnocchi and cook about 4 minutes, until tender. Stir in ½ (16 oz.) pkg. frozen peas *(thawed)*, ¼ C. whipping cream, and salt and black pepper to taste. Add ½ C. each shredded Pepper Jack and cheddar cheeses; stir until melted.

SHEET PAN MAC

Preheat the oven to 425° and line a rimmed 10 x 15" baking sheet with parchment paper. Cook 12 oz. pasta *(we used ditalini)* according to package directions, 2 minutes less than al dente; drain.

In the empty pasta saucepan, melt 4 T. butter over medium heat. Add ¼ C. flour and whisk for 1 minute. Whisk in 1¼ tsp. salt, ½ tsp. black pepper, and 2 C. each milk and chicken broth; bring to a boil, then reduce heat and simmer for 20 minutes, until it thickens a bit, whisking often. Remove from the heat and add ¾ C. each shredded Parmesan and Romano cheeses; whisk until melted.

Stir in the cooked pasta and pour evenly into the prepped baking sheet. Top with 8 oz. sliced fresh mozzarella cheese. Mix 4 T. melted butter, 3 C. fresh bread crumbs, 1½ tsp. minced garlic, ¼ tsp. salt, and a handful of chopped fresh parsley; sprinkle over the pasta and bake for 25 minutes, until golden brown.

27

SERVES 8

MAC & CHEESE-CRUSTED PIZZA

1 (7.25 oz.) pkg. macaroni & cheese dinner mix, plus butter & milk needed for preparing

2 eggs, lightly beaten

½ lb. bulk Italian sausage

½ green bell pepper, chopped

⅓ C. chopped onion

1 (8 oz.) can pizza sauce

About 12 cherry tomatoes, halved

1 C. shredded mozzarella cheese

½ C. shredded Asiago cheese

Fresh basil

Preheat the oven to 375°. Prepare the macaroni & cheese dinner mix according to package directions; stir in eggs. Spread out mixture to make a 12" circle on a greased pizza pan. Bake for 15 minutes or until set and light brown. Remove the pan, but don't turn off the oven.

Meanwhile in a skillet, cook the sausage, bell pepper, and onion over medium heat until meat is no longer pink, breaking up sausage as it cooks; drain.

Spread the pizza sauce over the pasta crust. Top with the drained sausage mixture, tomatoes, and both cheeses. Bake for 10 to 12 minutes or until the cheese is melted. Toss on basil before serving.

CARAMELIZED ONION & SWISS

¼ C. olive oil, divided

3 yellow onions

12 oz. uncooked pasta *(we used rigatoni)*

3 T. butter

¼ C. flour

1 C. each milk & beef broth

2 tsp. salt

½ tsp. black pepper

2½ C. shredded Swiss cheese, divided

¼ C. Ritz cracker crumbs

2 tsp. dried thyme

In a large skillet, heat 2 tablespoons oil over medium heat. Cut onions lengthwise into ¼" slices and add them to the skillet. Sauté for 45 minutes or until they have softened, browned, and cooked down to about 2 cups, stirring occasionally; set aside.

Preheat the oven to 350° and grease a 9 x 13" baking pan. Cook pasta to al dente according to package directions; rinse with cold water, drain, and set aside.

In the meantime, in a medium saucepan over medium heat, melt the butter; whisk in the flour, milk, broth, salt, and black pepper. Cook until the sauce thickens, whisking constantly. Remove from the heat and add 1 cup of the cheese, whisking until melted.

Stir together the cooked pasta, caramelized onions, and cheese sauce; pour into the prepped pan.

Stir together the cracker crumbs, thyme, remaining 2 tablespoons oil, and remaining 1½ cups cheese; sprinkle over the pasta mixture. Bake for 20 to 25 minutes or until heated through and topping is golden brown.

SMOKY MAC & 'MATERS

Preheat the oven to broil. In a medium saucepan, cook 8 oz. pasta *(we used garden rotini)* according to package directions; drain and set aside.

In the empty pasta saucepan, melt 1½ T. butter over medium-low heat and stir in 1 T. flour. Add 1 C. milk, whisking until it starts to thicken. Slowly add ¾ C. shredded smoked provolone cheese, 8 oz. cubed Velveeta cheese, and ½ C. shredded Gruyère cheese, stirring until melted; stir in cooked pasta.

Hollow out 8 big tomatoes, season inside with salt and black pepper, and set in a rimmed baking pan; fill tomatoes with pasta mixture. Top with crushed potato chips and broil for 1 to 2 minutes, until toasted.

BROWN BUTTER-SAUSAGE ALFREDO

Cook 8 oz. pasta *(we used extra wide homemade-style egg noodles)* according to package directions; drain. In the meantime, slice 3 Italian sausage links and brown in a large skillet; drain. Set all aside.

In the empty skillet, melt ¼ C. butter and let it simmer for a few minutes until golden brown; grate 1 clove garlic into the butter and cook 30 seconds longer. Stir in 1 C. heavy cream and 1 C. grated Asiago cheese until melted. Stir in set-aside pasta and sausage; season with salt and black pepper. Sprinkle with fresh parsley, basil, and/or oregano before serving.

SERVES 6

SPINACH & ARTICHOKE

1 (10 oz.) pkg. frozen spinach, thawed

1 (14 oz.) can artichoke hearts, drained, rinsed & coarsely chopped

4 oz. cream cheese, softened

1 C. shredded Parmesan cheese, divided

1 chopped green onion

2 T. minced garlic, divided

1 C. panko bread crumbs

12 oz. uncooked pasta *(we used whole wheat penne)*

3 T. butter

3 T. flour

2 C. milk

1 tsp. dry mustard

¼ tsp. black pepper

1 C. each shredded cheddar & Havarti cheeses

1 T. Sriracha sauce

½ C. dry white wine

Squeeze the spinach in a towel to remove all excess liquid; put the spinach in a bowl with the artichoke hearts, cream cheese, and ½ cup Parmesan cheese. Stir in the green onion and 1 tablespoon garlic. Heat the bread crumbs in a dry skillet until light golden brown. Set all aside.

Cook pasta according to package directions; drain. In the meantime, melt the butter over medium heat; whisk in the flour until golden brown. Slowly whisk in the milk and bring to a boil. Remove the pan from the heat; stir in the dry mustard, black pepper, and the remaining 1 tablespoon garlic. Add the cheddar and Havarti cheeses, a handful at a time, and the remaining ½ cup Parmesan cheese, stirring until melted. Stir in the Sriracha sauce, wine, the set-aside spinach mixture, and the cooked pasta.

Sprinkle set-aside bread crumbs over the top before serving.

BUFFALO M&C PIZZA

1 large chicken breast half, cut into bite-size pieces

¼ C. cornstarch

Salt & coarse black pepper to taste

2 C. canola oil

Hot sauce to taste

12 oz. uncooked pasta *(we used casarecce)*

2 T. butter

2 T. flour

2 C. milk

8 oz. shredded cheddar cheese

1 (11 oz.) roll refrigerated pizza crust

1 C. shredded provolone cheese

½ C. crumbled blue cheese

1 celery rib, finely chopped

Set a baking pan or pizza pan in the oven; preheat the oven and the pan to 500°. Put the chicken pieces into a bowl with the cornstarch, and season with salt and pepper; toss to coat.

In a deep-fryer, heat the oil to 350°. In batches, fry the chicken in the hot oil for 5 to 7 minutes or until golden brown. Use a slotted spoon to remove the chicken from the fryer and set on paper towels to drain. Dump the drained chicken into a clean bowl and stir in hot sauce until coated; set aside.

Cook pasta according to package directions, 1 minute less than al dente; drain and return to the saucepan. In the meantime, melt the butter in a separate saucepan and whisk in the flour until golden. Slowly whisk in the milk and cook until thickened, whisking constantly; remove from the heat. Add the cheddar cheese, a little at a time, and stir until melted. Pour the cheese sauce into the cooked pasta and give it a good stir. Season with salt and black pepper.

Remove the hot pan from the oven *(don't forget to use an oven mitt)*, coat with cooking spray, and very carefully press the pizza dough onto the pan. Top the dough with the provolone cheese, pasta mixture, fried chicken, and blue cheese.

Bake for 15 minutes or until the crust is golden brown and the topping is bubbly. Sprinkle the celery over the top before serving. And if you like things really hot, go ahead and drizzle on some more hot sauce.

CHEESY STUFFED PORTOBELLOS

3 large portobello mushrooms, stems removed

½ C. red wine, plus more for drizzling

1 tsp. minced garlic

2 C. leftover macaroni & cheese (*we used Caramelized Onion & Swiss, page 30*)

¼ C. grated Romano cheese, divided

1½ tsp. chopped fresh parsley

1 green onion, sliced

Preheat the oven to 400°. Scrape out most of the gills from the inside of each mushroom cap, leaving those around the outside intact to help support the lip.

Bring ½ cup wine and the garlic to a simmer over medium heat in an oven-safe skillet. Place the mushrooms in the skillet, stem side up, and divide the prepared macaroni & cheese among them; sprinkle with 3 tablespoons Romano cheese. Bake for 10 to 15 minutes, until heated through.

Remove the mushrooms from the oven (*don't forget to use an oven mitt*) and top each with some parsley, green onion, and remaining cheese. Drizzle with a little more wine, if you'd like.

REUBEN BOWLS

8 oz. uncooked pasta *(we used pipette)*

2 T. olive oil, divided

1 onion, chopped

Salt & black pepper

½ tsp. minced garlic

1 T. flour

1½ C. half & half

4 oz. cream cheese, cubed

3 T. Dijon mustard

¼ tsp. each ground nutmeg & cayenne pepper

8 oz. each shredded Gruyère & sharp cheddar cheeses

1 (8 oz.) can sauerkraut, drained

8 oz. deli corned beef, chopped

4 slices marbled pumpernickel rye bread, crusts removed

Set a rimmed baking sheet in the oven; preheat the oven and baking sheet to 425°. Grease six individual ramekins. Cook pasta according to package directions; drain. Set all aside.

In the meantime, in a large saucepan over medium-low heat, heat 1 tablespoon oil. Add the onion, ¾ teaspoon salt, and ¼ teaspoon black pepper. Cover and cook for 8 to 10 minutes or until very tender and lightly browned, stirring occasionally. Stir in the garlic and cook for 1 minute. Sprinkle the flour over the onion mixture, stir, and cook 1 minute longer. Whisk in the half & half and bring to a simmer. Then add the cream cheese, mustard, nutmeg, and cayenne pepper, stirring until melted and well blended. Stir in the Gruyère and cheddar cheeses and simmer until melted, stirring occasionally.

Toss the cooked pasta into the cheese sauce, stir in the sauerkraut and corned beef, and divide the mixture evenly among the prepped ramekins.

Cube the bread and toss into a small bowl. Stir in ¼ teaspoon each salt and black pepper, and the remaining 1 tablespoon oil. Divide the cubes among the ramekins and bake for 10 to 12 minutes or until golden brown.

HOT COWBOY MAC

16 oz. uncooked pasta
(*we used rigatoni*)

3 T. butter

2 cloves garlic, minced

½ tsp. dry mustard

1½ to 2 T. chipotle pepper
sauce

3 T. flour

1¼ C. vegetable broth

1½ C. plus 2 T. milk

1½ C. each shredded
Pepper Jack & sharp
cheddar cheeses

Black pepper & crushed
red pepper flakes to taste

3 (15.5 oz.) cans chili
beans

Jalapeño peppers, sliced &
seeded, optional

Cook pasta to al dente according to package directions; drain and set aside.

In the meantime, in a big saucepan, melt the butter over medium heat. Stir in the garlic, dry mustard, and pepper sauce, cooking until fragrant. Sprinkle in the flour and whisk for 1 minute. Slowly whisk in the broth and milk. Bring to a simmer and cook about 10 minutes or until smooth and slightly thickened.

Remove the pan from the heat and whisk in both cheeses until melted and smooth. Season with black pepper and red pepper flakes. Toss in the cooked pasta and stir so every bite is nice and cheesy.

Heat the beans briefly. Serve the cheesy pasta over the beans, and top with jalapeños if you'd like extra heat.

CHEESE-STEAK SOUP

12 to 16 oz. uncooked pasta *(we used extra wide egg noodles)*

¾ C. frozen peas

2 T. butter

½ lb. sirloin steak, cut into small pieces

1½ C. diced onion

¾ C. each diced celery & carrots

¼ C. flour

3 T. Dijon mustard

6 C. beef broth

1 C. each shredded Muenster & Gruyère cheeses

¾ C. each shredded Parmesan & Monterey Jack cheeses

¼ tsp. ground nutmeg

Salt & black pepper to taste

¾ C. heavy cream or milk

Cook pasta according to package directions, adding peas during the last 2 minutes of cooking time; drain, rinse with cold water, and set aside.

In the empty pasta saucepan, melt the butter over medium heat. Add the steak, onion, celery, and carrots, cooking until vegetables are soft and steak is no longer pink. Reduce heat to low, stir in flour and mustard, and cook 2 to 3 minutes longer. Stir in the broth, bring to a simmer, and heat until mixture begins to thicken.

Add all the cheese, a handful at a time, stirring until melted. Stir in the nutmeg, salt, black pepper, and cream; simmer for 5 minutes. Just before serving, stir in cooked pasta and peas.

ROASTED GARLIC, KALE & BACON

1 garlic bulb*

Olive oil, optional

16 oz. uncooked pasta *(we used whole wheat farfalle)*

3 T. butter

½ onion, diced

¼ C. flour

3 C. milk

8 oz. shredded sharp white cheddar cheese

2 T. grated Parmesan cheese

Dash each ground nutmeg & cayenne pepper

½ tsp. salt

¼ tsp. black pepper

½ lb. bacon, cooked & crumbled

¼ lb. fresh kale, trimmed & chopped

1 C. crushed garlic croutons

Preheat the oven to 425°. Keeping the garlic bulb intact, slice off about ½" of the top so that a little of each individual clove has been removed. Set the bulb on foil and drizzle olive oil into the bulb until the oil just begins to overflow. Wrap the foil tightly around the bulb and set it in a small baking pan; bake for 35 minutes. Squeeze the bulb over a small bowl to release all the garlic; mash with a fork and set aside.

Reduce the oven temperature to 375°. Cook pasta to al dente according to package directions; drain and set aside.

Meanwhile, in a big saucepan, melt the butter over medium heat. Add the onion and cook 5 minutes or until tender and golden. Sprinkle in the flour and whisk for a minute. Slowly whisk in the milk and cook until just starting to thicken, whisking occasionally. Toss in both cheeses, a handful at a time, whisking until melted and creamy. Stir in the nutmeg, cayenne pepper, salt, black pepper, roasted garlic, bacon, kale, and cooked pasta.

Transfer the pasta mixture to a greased 9 x 13" baking pan and sprinkle with croutons. Bake for 15 minutes.

* While you're at it, you might want to consider roasting a couple of extra garlic bulbs to store in an airtight container in the fridge for other recipes.

SERVES 6

SKILLET LASAGNA

8 oz. uncooked pasta
  (we used mafalda)

1 lb. lean ground beef

¼ C. chopped onion

1 (24 oz.) jar spaghetti
  sauce

1 (16 oz.) container
  cottage cheese

8 oz. shredded mozzarella
  cheese

Grated Parmesan cheese,
  optional

Cook the pasta to al dente according to package directions; drain. In the meantime, in a big skillet, cook the beef and onion until the beef is no longer pink, breaking it apart as it cooks; drain and return to the skillet.

Stir half the spaghetti sauce into the cooked beef and spread it out over the bottom of the skillet. Spread the cottage cheese over the meat mixture, and then add the cooked pasta in an even layer. Drizzle on the remaining sauce and top with the mozzarella cheese.

Cover the pan and cook a few minutes, until the cheese melts. Sprinkle on Parmesan cheese before serving, if you'd like.

LEMON & BRUSSELS SPROUTS

Cook 12 oz. pasta *(we used orecchiette)* to al dente according to package directions; drain. In the empty pasta saucepan, heat 1½ T. olive oil over medium heat and add 1 tsp. minced garlic; cook for 30 seconds. Add 12 oz. thinly sliced or shredded fresh Brussels sprouts, 1 T. crushed red pepper flakes, and a pinch of salt; cook 5 minutes, stirring often.

Stir in 6 oz. mascarpone cheese, ¾ C. heavy cream, 1 C. milk, and 3 oz. goat cheese, stirring until melted. Stir in 1 tsp. lemon zest and 3 T. lemon juice. Mix with the cooked pasta.

DUMP & GO
SLOW COOKER MAC

Pour ½ C. melted butter into a slow cooker; brush it around to grease the sides and leave the remainder in the cooker. Turn the cooker to the low setting. Dump in 16 oz. uncooked pasta *(we used elbows)*, 1 (5 oz.) can evaporated milk, 2 C. milk, 1 (10.75 oz.) can cheddar cheese soup, and salt and black pepper to taste.

Beat 2 eggs and pour them into the cooker; add 2 C. shredded cheddar cheese. Stir it all up, cover the cooker, and walk away for 1½ hours.

Sprinkle 2 C. shredded Asiago cheese over the pasta, cover, and cook an additional 30 minutes to 1 hour, until the pasta is tender. Serve in bread bowls, if you'd like.

WACKY WALKING TACOS

1 onion, diced

1 T. vegetable oil

1 T. minced garlic

1 lb. ground beef

1 pint cherry tomatoes

1 C. water

2 C. beef broth

8 oz. uncooked pasta
(we used cellentani)

2 tsp. each ground cumin & chili powder

1 tsp. each salt & black pepper

2 C. shredded cheddar cheese

6 individual bags Doritos or Fritos corn chips

Your favorite taco toppings

In a big saucepan, cook the onion in hot oil until soft. Then toss in garlic and cook 30 seconds longer. Add the ground beef to the saucepan and cook until no longer pink, breaking it up as it cooks; drain and return to the pan.

Dice the cherry tomatoes and add them to the drained ground beef. Add water, broth, pasta, cumin, chili powder, salt, and black pepper; bring to a boil, cover, and cook for 15 minutes, stirring often.

Uncover the saucepan and continue cooking until the liquid is absorbed. Remove the saucepan from the heat and add the cheese, stirring until melted.

Spoon the mixture into bags of Doritos or Fritos, stirring until well blended. Add your favorite toppings, grab a fork, and dig in!

TEX-MEX

2 poblano peppers

2 ears fresh sweet corn

8 oz. uncooked pasta
(we used elbows)

½ C. ground sausage or
chopped chorizo

6 T. butter, divided

3 T. flour

1½ C. milk

12 oz. beer

3½ C. shredded Pepper
Jack cheese

1 tsp. salt

¼ tsp. black pepper

¾ C. crushed tortilla chips

¼ C. panko bread crumbs

Grease a casserole dish or six individual ramekins; set aside.

Grill the peppers and corn on a greased rack over medium heat until the peppers are blistered and the corn is lightly charred, turning occasionally.

Place the charred peppers in a zippered plastic freezer bag or a brown paper bag; close the bag tightly and set aside for 10 minutes. Then, remove the peppers from the bag, peel off and discard the skins and seeds, and chop the peppers. Cut the corn kernels off the cob. Set all aside. Preheat the oven to 400°.

Cook the pasta to al dente according to package directions; drain and rinse with cold water. Meanwhile, cook the sausage until no longer pink, breaking the meat apart while it cooks; drain. Set all aside.

Melt 3 tablespoons butter in the empty pasta saucepan over medium heat; whisk in the flour until smooth, cooking for 2 minutes until golden brown, whisking constantly. Slowly whisk in the milk and beer; cook for 10 to 15 minutes until thickened, whisking occasionally. Remove the pan from the heat and gradually add the cheese, stirring until melted. Stir in the chopped peppers, corn kernels, and cooked sausage; season with salt and black pepper. Carefully stir in the cooked pasta. Transfer the mixture to the prepped casserole dish.

Melt the remaining 3 tablespoons butter; stir in the tortilla chips and bread crumbs, and sprinkle over the pasta mixture. Bake for 12 to 15 minutes or until golden brown and bubbly.

GRILLED MAC & CHEE-EESY 'WICHES

1 C. uncooked pasta
(we used ziti)

Butter, softened

1 T. flour

½ C. milk

2 oz. cream cheese

½ C. each shredded
cheddar, Asiago &
Romano cheeses

8 slices Italian or
sourdough bread

2 to 3 oz. prosciutto or
Canadian bacon

Cook pasta according to package directions; drain and
set aside.

In a medium saucepan over medium heat, melt 1 tablespoon
butter. Whisk in flour until well combined. Gradually whisk
in milk and cook 1 to 2 minutes, until smooth, whisking
constantly. Stir in the cream cheese until melted, then add
all the cheese, a handful at a time, stirring until smooth.
Remove from the heat and stir in the cooked pasta until
well combined.

Butter one side of each bread slice. On the unbuttered side
of half the bread, layer the prosciutto and ¼ of the pasta
mixture. Top with another slice of bread, buttered side up.

Heat a griddle over medium heat and add the sandwiches;
fry until bread is golden and the filling is heated through,
flipping once to brown both sides.

KING RANCH CHICKEN

8 oz. uncooked pasta
(we used elbows)

1 onion

½ each red & green bell
pepper

2 T. butter

1 (10 oz.) can diced
tomatoes with green
chiles

8 oz. Velveeta, cubed

3 C. chopped cooked
chicken

1 (10.7 oz.) can cream
of chicken soup

½ C. sour cream

1 tsp. chili powder

½ tsp. ground cumin

¾ C. each shredded
Muenster & sharp
cheddar cheeses

Preheat the oven to 350°. Cook the pasta according to
package directions; drain and set aside. Coarsely chop the
onion and bell peppers.

In a large oven-proof skillet, melt the butter over medium-
high heat. Add the chopped onion and bell peppers and cook
for 5 minutes, until just tender. Stir in the tomatoes with
green chiles and the Velveeta; cook for 2 minutes or until the
cheese is melted, stirring constantly. Stir in the chicken, soup,
sour cream, chili powder, and cumin. Then, stir in the cooked
pasta until well blended.

Sprinkle the shredded cheeses over the top. Bake for
10 to 15 minutes or until the cheese melts.

SERVES 6

FRIED MAC & BACON BALLS

8 oz. uncooked pasta
  (we used elbows)

2 bacon strips

1 T. butter

1½ tsp. flour

1 C. milk

¼ tsp. salt

1¼ tsp. black pepper,
  divided

¼ tsp. cayenne pepper

6 oz. cheddar cheese
  curds

Vegetable oil for frying

2 or 3 eggs

½ C. panko bread crumbs

½ C. Italian-seasoned
  bread crumbs

½ tsp. garlic powder

Marinara, Alfredo sauce,
  or salsa, optional

Cook pasta according to package directions; drain. In the meantime, in a large skillet over medium heat, fry the bacon until crispy; drain, crumble, and set aside. Keep 1 tablespoon bacon drippings in the pan and discard the remainder.

Add the butter to the drippings in the pan and melt over medium heat. Whisk in the flour until well blended, then slowly whisk in the milk; bring to a boil. Stir in salt, ¼ teaspoon black pepper, cayenne pepper, and cheese curds. Reduce heat to medium-low and stir until cheese is melted. Stir in the crumbled bacon and cooked pasta. Transfer mixture to a greased 9 x 9" pan and refrigerate 2 to 3 hours.

With greased hands, shape the chilled pasta into compact 2" balls and place them in a single layer in a big pan; cover and freeze 3 hours.

Heat oil in a deep-fryer to 350°. In a shallow bowl, beat eggs with 1 tablespoon water. Place all the bread crumbs in another shallow bowl and stir in the garlic powder and the remaining 1 teaspoon black pepper. Coat the frozen balls with the egg and then the crumbs. Carefully lower a few at a time into the hot oil, frying 5 minutes or until golden brown and hot throughout; drain on paper towels.

Serve immediately with marinara, Alfredo sauce, or salsa, if you'd like.

MAC-STYLE JALAPEÑO POPPERS

10 large jalapeño peppers

1 C. uncooked pasta
(we used ditalini)

¼ C. milk

4 oz. Velveeta cheese,
cubed

2 to 3 T. ranch dressing,
plus more for serving

Salt & black pepper to
taste

2 C. Cheetos

Cooking spray

2 green onions, sliced

Preheat the oven to 350° and grease a rimmed baking sheet. Cut the peppers in half lengthwise and remove the seeds. Arrange the pepper halves on the prepped baking sheet and set aside.

Cook pasta according to package directions; drain and return to pan. Set the pan over low heat and add the milk, Velveeta, and 2 to 3 tablespoons ranch dressing, stirring until the cheese is melted.

Mound the pasta mixture evenly into the pepper halves. Season with salt and black pepper.

Put the Cheetos in a zippered plastic bag; close the bag, coarsely crush the Cheetos, and sprinkle them over the filled peppers. Spritz lightly with cooking spray. Bake for 15 minutes or until peppers are hot. Sprinkle with green onions and serve with more ranch dressing.

INDEX